Dear Readers,

As a mom to three daughters, one of my fondest memories is sharing the magic of reading with my girls, and I hope this book can bring joy and happiness to your home – like so many books did to ours.

During my college years, I was a cheerleader for the University of Georgia. One of the things I loved most about cheerleading was the selflessness of the sport. At its root, it is about championing others and energizing a crowd to see what is special about your team. As First Lady, my job is similar in a lot of ways. I can say without question that I have the very best team to celebrate: the great state of Georgia.

As you experience this book, you will see many of my favorite things about our beloved Peach State. Things like my love for Georgia's natural resources, including golden beaches that provide a safe haven for sea turtles to hatch and find their way to the sea and hike-able mountains that welcome millions of visitors.

You will also read about Georgia Grown products. Brian and I are always encouraging Georgia citizens to buy products, food, and materials that are locally grown and sourced. Supporting our farmers and small businesses is important to the economy of our state and the livelihoods of the farm families who produce these items.

Finally, this book touches on themes like love and respect for both people and our furry friends. At the Governor's Mansion, we host Pet Adoption Days, because everyone deserves a warm and loving home.

I am enthusiatic about collaborating with Malcolm and Chandler, two of my favorite Georgians, to bring you a book that I hope inspires kindness, self-worth, compassion, and encourages a positive dialogue in your homes and classrooms about all the wonderful things Georgia has to offer.

Happy reading,

Marty A. Kemp

TO THE STATE OF GEORGIA,

THank YOU.

- M.K.   - M.M   - C.F.

This book is a work of fiction. Names, characters, places, and incidents are either the product of the author's imagination or
are used fictitiously, and any resemblance to actual persons, living or dead, business establishments, events, or locales is
entirely coincidental. · American Program Bureau, Inc. can bring the author to your live event. For more information or to book
an event, contact the American Program Bureau, Inc. at 1-617-614-1600 or visit website https://www.apbspeakers.com.
Library of Congress Cataloging-in-Publication Data available
ISBN: 978-1-7923-1272-4
Printed in U.S.A. · First edition, March 2022

Book design by Dana Hrabovsky · The text type was set in Chelsea Market Pro and Chinchilla.
The layout was set in Adobe InDesign and Adobe Illustrator. The illustrations were created on canvas. Digital edits were made.

MALCOLM MITCHELL

HEY, GEORGIA

ILLUSTRATED BY
CHANDLER FOWLER

INSPIRED BY
FIRST LADY
MARTY KEMP

For the record,

I know
the names
of all
my states.

Want me
to prove it?

Watch
and
See.

two

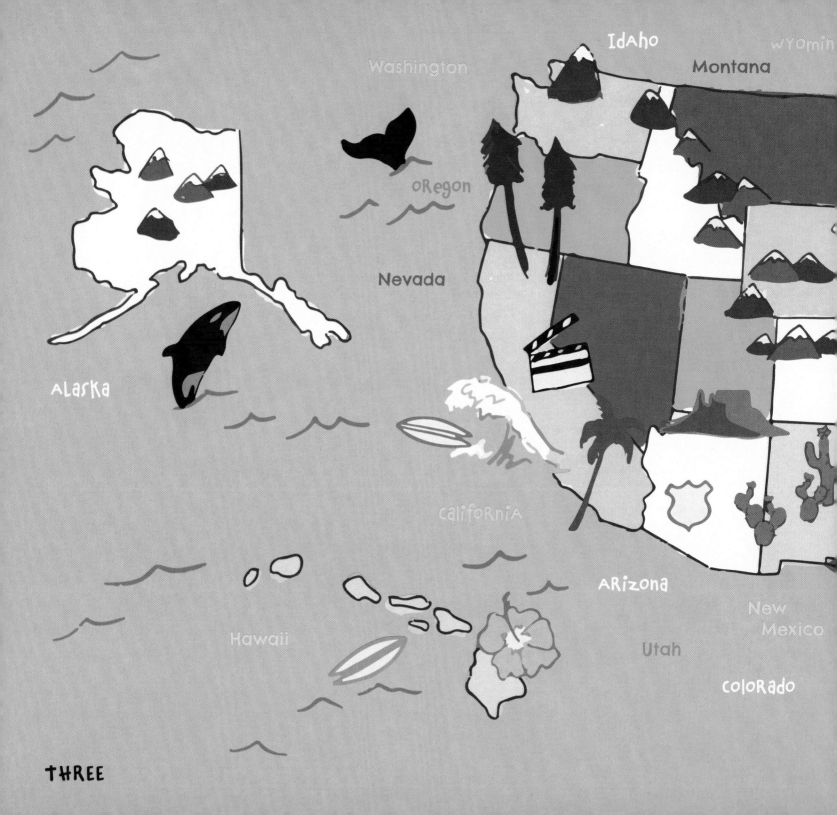

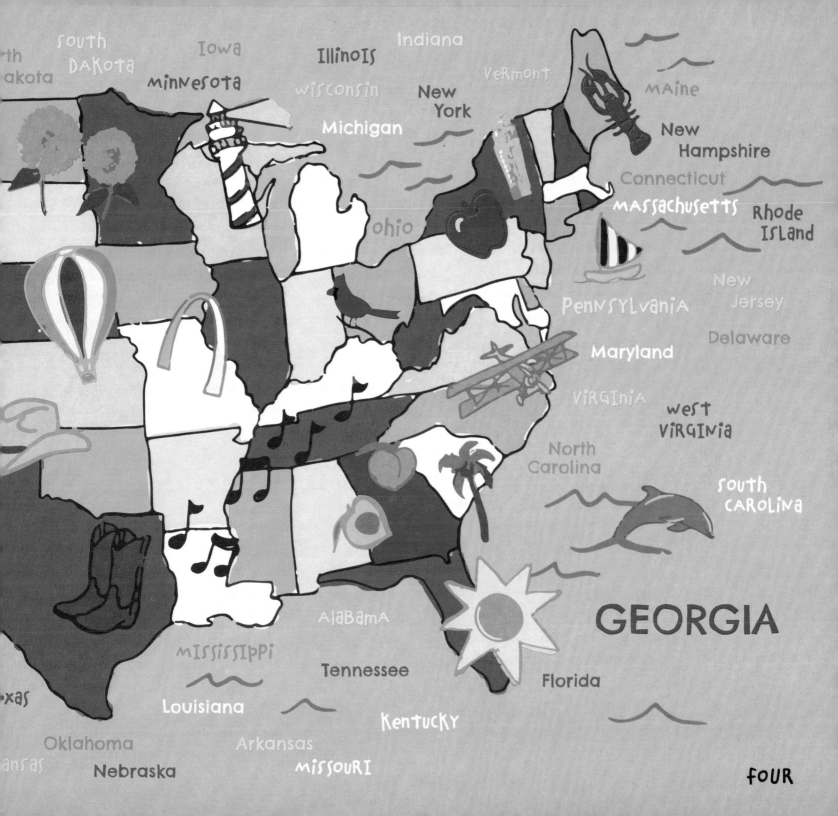

FIVE

I think all
the states are
cool and special,
but I cheer
loudest, proudest,
and rowdiest
for GEORGIA,
the place where I live.

I bet you think I am being silly willy about GEORGIA being super, but it is true.

We have...

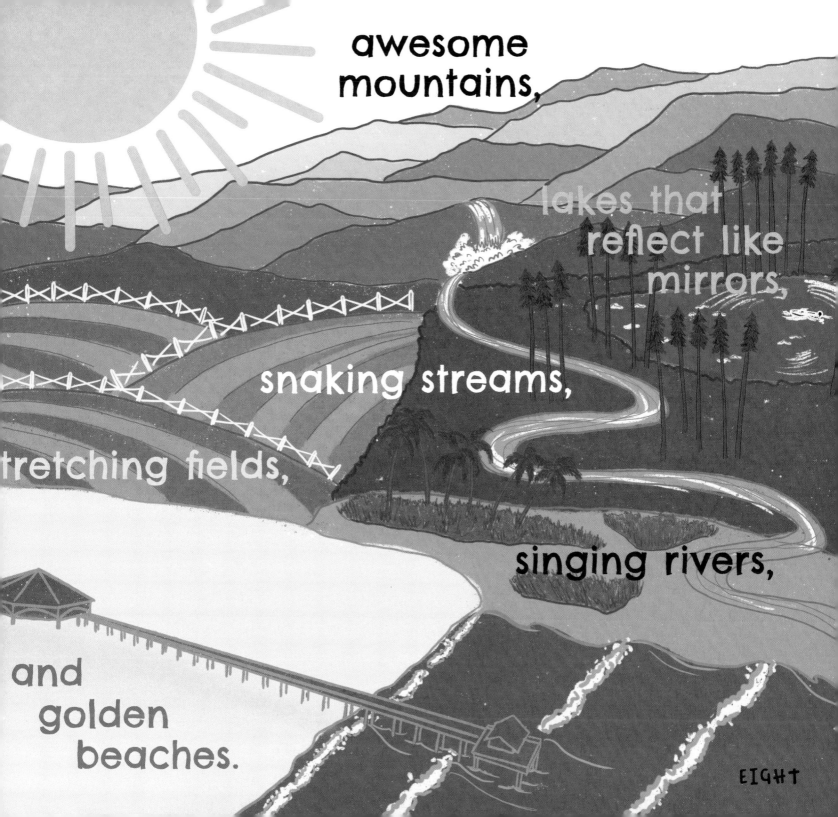

We have the best

bulldogs, wildcats, sweet bumblebees, giant trees, fuzzy peaches, boiled peanuts, deviled eggs, pecan pie, baby red birds, and even a museum packed with lunchboxes.

GEORGIA
is the best.

I love cheering for my state, but there are things you and I can do to make it even better. I know if we cheer hard for GEORGIA, we can make amazing things happen.

ELEVEN

TWELVE

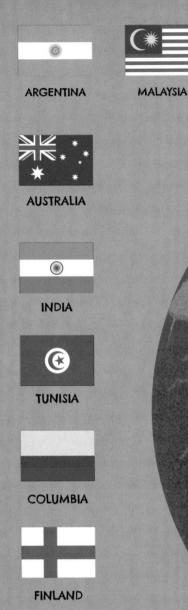

ARGENTINA MALAYSIA NORWAY ALGERIA SWITZERLAND SOUTH KOREA IRELAND CANAD

AUSTRALIA

CUBA

INDIA

EGYP

TUNISIA

POLAN

COLUMBIA

PHILLIPP

FINLAND

CHIN

PERU

HUNGA

JAPAN QATAR NIGERIA IRAN RUSSIA BELGIUM TURKEY GREE

RMANY
 UNITED KINGDOM
 SAUDI ARABIA
 ISRAEL
 KAZAKHSTAN
 SOUTH AFRICA
 ITALY
USA

 .GARIA
SWEDEN

 EZUELA
SPAIN

 RAQ
MEXICO

 STRIA
NETHERLANDS

 ZEALAND
ROMANIA

 JGUAY
CHILE

If you and I agree to give it a kid-tastic effort until our socks fly off, I know,

cheering for GEORGIA could change the whole world.

 ANCE
 BRAZIL
 DENMARK
THAILAND
 INDONESIA
 UKRAINE
 PORTUGAL
 LEBANON

More love,
less hate.

That is a great way
to protect our state.

Negatives become positives.

That is how frowns
turn upside down.
And what does
an upside down
frown make?
A smile.

NINETEEN

Right is right,
and
wrong is wrong.

We can disagree and still get along.

TWENTY

KaLeiDOsc

A

That is what GEORGIA
can be:

filled with HAPPY COLORS

O pe

vesOme

and FUN shapes

make it and CLeaR.

POWERFUL AS A falcon,

BRAVE AS A Hawk.

TWENTY FOUR

TWENTY FIVE

TWENTY SIX

TWENTY SEVEN

TWENTY EIGHT

malcolm mitchell

Malcolm Mitchell, Super Bowl Champion and literacy crusader, was born in Valdosta, Georgia and graduated from the University of Georgia with a degree in Communication Studies in 2015. After his career in the National Football League (NFL), Malcolm turned his full attention to enriching young lives through writing relevant stories for children, like *The Magician's Hat* and *My Very Favorite Book in the Whole Wide World*, and leading his Share the Magic Foundation. In *Hey, GEORGIA*, Malcolm hopes to connect with his home state and share a message that we are better together.

Email: info@readwithmalcolm
Social Media: @readwithmalcolm
Website: www.readwithmalcolm.com

chandler fowler

Chandler Fowler was raised in Savannah, Georgia and graduated from Savannah Arts Academy as a visual arts major. In 2020, she graduated from the University of Georgia with a Bachelor of Arts in Interdisciplinary Art and Design and minors in Studio Art and Communication Studies. Since graduation, Chandler has become a freelance artist and graphic designer and now resides in Austin, Texas.

Email: chandlerfowlerdesign@gmail.com
Social Media: @chandlerfowlerdesign
Website: www.chandlerfowler.com